W9-CCD-505

Nevada
impressions

FARCOUNTRY
PRESS

photography by Scott T. Smith

Front cover: Golden sand and tumbleweeds contrast with the deep blue of Walker Lake, unique in the desert for supporting a substantial fishery.

Back cover: Found only in the Mojave Desert, the Joshua tree is not a tree at all, but a member of the yucca family.

Title page: The Reese River flows past rabbitbrush in late spring while snow still covers the peaks of the Toiyabe Range.

Right: Also known as Spanish daggers for their bayonetlike leaves, Mojave yucca plants punctuate the *bajadas* in the Meadow Valley Mountains.

ISBN1-56037-308-3
Photography © 2004 by Scott T. Smith
© 2004 Farcountry Press

This book may not be reproduced in whole or in part by any means (with the exception of short quotes for the purpose of review) without the permission of the publisher.

For more information about our books write Farcountry Press, P.O. Box 5630, Helena, MT 59604; call (800) 821-3874; or visit www.farcountrypress.com.

Created, produced, and designed in the United States.
Printed in China.

Right: Fort Churchill State Historic Park preserves the ruins of a U.S. Army fort built to provide protection for early settlers. Constructed in 1861, it was abandoned only nine years later.

Facing page: Sagebrush abounds in the Goshute Mountains. Nevada's state flower, it easily can be identified by its sharp odor—a mixture of turpentine and camphor. Some Native American tribes used its leaves as medicine and its bark for weaving mats.

Left: Abundant throughout Nevada—and the most widely distributed tree species in North America—aspen trees offer stunning fall color. The nickname of "quaking aspen" comes from the fact that its leaves are perpendicular to their stems, thus offering a flat surface to wind from any direction.

Facing page: The Blue Lakes were formed after a mountain glacier melted, leaving a large depression (a cirque) that was then filled by springs from the surrounding hillside. Other nearby evidence of glaciation includes polished rock, moraines, and striation.

Right: Roads in Nevada often run straight as far as the eye can see, like this stretch of Nevada Highway 359 near Whiskey Flat. The Nevada segment of U.S. Route 50 is known by many as the loneliest highway in America.

Below: People thrill to see migratory Canada geese fly overhead in signature "V" formations as they honk their way across the skies of the Truckee Meadows. Many geese stay year-round in the Reno–Sparks area due to lush lawns and golf courses, plentiful lakes and ponds (such as this one at the University of Nevada, Reno), and the absence of shotgun blasts.

Facing page: The Mojave yucca is often confused with its cousin, the Joshua tree. But when they are found together (as they often are), it is easy to identify the Joshua tree, which can grow to 25 feet or more and often forms "forests."

Above: Desert sailors utilize dry lake beds just as willingly as wet ones.

Facing page: New York–New York Hotel and Casino in Las Vegas showcases twelve adjoining skyscraper towers, which architecturally recreate at one-third scale some of the most famous New York City skyscrapers—plenty of rooms for the city's 35 million annual visitors.

A stunning sight on private property in the Black Rock Desert is Fly Geyser, born in 1964 when a geo-thermal company drilled a test well searching for places to tap steam-gener-ated power. When the well was not properly plugged, superheated groundwater con-tinued to spout from the ground. The characteristic bright red and green are caused by a type of algae that flourishes in high temperatures.

Left: Petroglyphs, found in many sites throughout Nevada, recall area residents from thousands of years ago.

Below: Belmont, which thrived from 1865 through 1885, produced some $15 million in silver and lead ore.

Facing page: The rugged, heavily wooded Goshute Mountains drain to fields of grasses in the lowlands. In spring, Indian paintbrush adds color to the landscape.

Above: Canyon country is famous for its "slot canyons," where your shoulders almost touch both sides at once. Anniversary Narrows in southern Nevada's Muddy Mountains is 400 to 600 feet deep but only 7 to 15 feet wide.

Facing page: Creosote bushes are widespread in hot deserts. The original bush can live to be 100 years old, but it clones genetically identical plants from its root system. This "clone family" can live for thousands of years, earning for the creosote the title of oldest living thing on earth.

Penstemon wildflowers and the white bark of aspen trees contrast sharply with the dark, rugged peaks (eight of which are over 10,000 feet) in the Jarbidge Wilderness.

A backpacker pauses on the middle summit of Mount Jefferson, the highest peak in central Nevada, to enjoy the stormy mixture of shadow and light. In 1978 a 7,000-year-old archeological site was discovered on the peak, the highest known Indian village in North America.

Right: The desert tortoise, Nevada's state reptile, is the "old man of the desert," living up to 100 years.

Below: The "Million Dollar Courthouse" in Pioche started in 1871 at a price of $16,400. However, with design changes, delayed payments, and mounting interest rates, local politicians managed to inflate the initial cost to about a million dollars, which was not paid off until 1936.

Facing page: During the Pleistocene era, which began about 1.6 million years ago, Lake Lahontan covered much of central and northern Nevada. As the climate dried, the lake receded and many closed valleys became isolated dry lake beds.

Above: The numerous valleys of Nevada have supported a vigorous cattle industry since the 1850s. Completion of the transcontinental railroad in 1869 created a prosperous industry. Longhorns from Texas were driven to fertile valleys for feeding then shipped as far as Omaha and San Francisco to market.

Right: Many of the old Basque sheepherder carvings on aspen trees date back to the 1930s.

Facing page: Lupine wildflowers adorn the meadows below Marys River Peak in the Humboldt National Forest.

23

Elephant Rock is typical of the whimsically named sandstone formations
at Valley of Fire, Nevada's oldest and largest state park.

Left: Llama packing has become increasingly popular in wilderness areas as a way of lightening the load without tearing up trails.

Below: Fireweed and red osier dogwood add fall color along Hendrys Creek in the Snake Range.

Ward Charcoal Ovens State Historic Park features six beehive-shaped ovens built in 1873 to generate charcoal for use in the smelters that processed silver from nearby mines. The parabolic shape reflected heat back into the center, and the ovens produced about 30 bushels of charcoal per cord of wood. It took 13 days to fill, burn, and empty a 35-cord kiln. The huge ovens are 30 feet high and 27 feet in diameter at the base, with 20-inch-thick walls.

Left: Lake Tahoe can be seen in the distance beyond wind-scoured snow patterns on the Mount Rose ridge crest.

Facing page: A clearing winter storm leaves snow-capped cliffs in the Red Rock Canyon National Conservation Area outside of Las Vegas.

Above: Hoover Dam, the largest dam of its time, was built during the Depression in less than five years—completed ahead of schedule and under budget. A National Historic Landmark, it is still a world-renowned structure taming the Colorado River and providing water, electrical power, flood control, and recreational benefits to the entire Southwest. PHOTO BY DEON REYNOLDS

Facing page: This lake at the head of the South Fork of Pine Creek is not only untamed, it is unnamed.

Above: From a dirt runway, a water well, and a small operations shack in 1941, Nellis Air Force Base has become known as the "Home of the Fighter Pilot." Since 1956 it has served as base of the Thunderbirds, an elite unit composed of 8 pilots, 4 support officers, 4 civilians, and about 120 enlisted people. The Thunderbirds' aerial demonstration, lasting over an hour, is a mix of formation flying and solo routines. PHOTO BY DEON REYNOLDS

Right: From the 13,063-foot summit of Wheeler Peak, the view is fantastic! But you must venture closer to see all the streams, lakes, alpine plants, abundant wildlife, variety of forest types, and numerous limestone caverns that are preserved in Great Basin National Park, set aside in 1986 as one of the newest national parks in the U.S.

Left: With Lakes Mead and Mohave as the central focus, visitors to Lake Mead National Recreation Area enjoy a wide variety of water recreation activities in a rugged and picturesque setting.

Below: Pinyon pines frame Troy Mountain.

Facing page: Lake Tahoe–Nevada State Park on a windy day.

Right: Beavertail cactus blooming among spring grasses and wildflowers.

Below: Barrel cactus grows among colorful sandstone slabs at Valley of Fire State Park.

Facing page: With some 200,000 residents in less than 100 square miles, the "biggest little city in the world" offers skiing, snowboarding, hiking, camping, golfing, and fishing, as well as world-famous gambling and shows.

Above: When it opened in 1876, Virginia City's Fourth Ward School was the finest of its kind on the West Coast. The elegant Victorian structure was designed to serve more than 1,000 students and featured a modern heating and ventilation system, interior flush toilets, drinking fountains, and single desks for each student. The school now serves as a museum.

Right: An autumn snow dusts the limestone ridgeline in the South Pequop Wilderness Study Area.

Facing page: Snags on the shore of Baker Lake reward the sunrise visitor to Great Basin National Park.

Above: Today, more than 90 percent of Nevada's cropland is devoted to feed for livestock.

Left: Volcanic pinnacles rise from canyon walls in the Jarbidge River Canyon.

Willows along the Reese River bottomland
contrast with winter snow.

Left: Genoa is the oldest permanent settlement in Nevada. Its bar, the oldest in the state, is in its third century of serving whiskey.

Below: Pronghorns are the fastest-running hoofed animal in North America. Adults have been clocked at 55 miles per hour. When alarmed, the white hairs on the rump patch are extended vertically, making the white visible for great distances.

Above: The Fountain of the Gods is modeled after the famous Trevi, which marked the center of the marketplace in Rome. At the Forum Shops adjacent to Caesars Palace, it still monitors shopping binges. PHOTO BY DEON REYNOLDS

Facing page: Isolated bushes on the playa in Railroad Valley, with the Grant Range in the distance.

Almost 18,000 wild horses and 1,500 burros—half of the nation's total—
live on Nevada rangelands managed by the Bureau of Land Management.

Surprisingly in the
arid desert, water has
been the primary
force sculpting the
sandstone in the
Muddy Mountains
of southern Nevada.

Right: Depending on the source, the Ruby Crest Trail varies from 32 to 40 miles. At any length, some of its hikers truly appreciate the help of llamas!

Below: Windmill and corral in Gabbs Valley.

Facing page: A bristlecone pine snag contrasts with the golden glow of aspen. Bristlecones are the longest-living tree on earth. The oldest ones usually grow at elevations of 10,000 to 11,000 feet and may have only a few strands of bark remaining in crevices, protected from sandblasting winds.

Above: Wildflowers at Greys Lake.

Facing page: Cirrus clouds above Ruby Mountains and a slough along Franklin Lake.

Right: Hiker in a narrow limestone canyon in the Arrow Canyon Range.

Facing page: Salmon Falls Creek emerges from a basalt gorge in the Badlands Wilderness Study Area.

When rains have been plentiful in the desert, valley floors can erupt with flowers such as these desert golds, desert primroses, and white-bracted stick-leaves.

Now a picnic area in Valley of Fire State Park, these historic stone cabins were built with native sandstone by the Civilian Conservation Corps in the 1930s to shelter passing travelers. PHOTO BY DEON REYNOLDS

Right: The Tuscarora cemetery dates from the town's golden years of 1870 to 1890 when its mines produced $40 million in silver. The town's population was about 4,000, split almost equally between whites and the Chinese who originally came to build the railroad. PHOTO BY DEON REYNOLDS

Below: The old Union Pacific Depot in Caliente, built in 1923, now houses city government offices and the library.

Facing page: Fog at Lunar Crater, a maar volcano listed on the National Natural Landmark Register.

Above: As the mining boom subsided, Nevada's ranches kept the state alive in the late nineteenth century.

Facing page: Clouds often lend drama to the exotic rock formations at Valley of Fire State Park.

The 32-acre reservoir at Cave Lake State Park is popular for trout fishing, boating, picnicking, and camping.

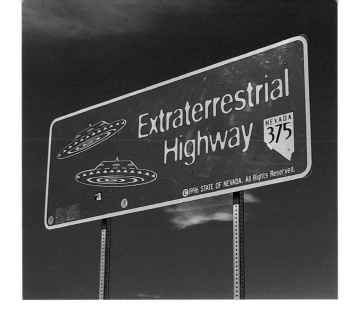

Above: In 1996, Governor Bob Miller officially renamed Nevada Highway 375. By design, the road's rechristening coincided with the release of *Independence Day*, Twentieth Century Fox's blockbuster movie about invading aliens. Of course, ever since the U.S. government created Area 51 in the late 1950s, the two-lane blacktop road has been a favored destination for UFO believers and skeptics alike.

PHOTO BY DEON REYNOLDS

Left: Fallen limber pine trees add textural beauty to the slope above Pine Creek in the Toquima Range.

Right: The Luxor Resort and Casino in Las Vegas was scrupulously researched for cultural and historical accuracy. Among other features, it offers a life-size replica of the Great Temple of Ramses II, and its King Tut's Tomb and Museum is the only full-scale authentic reproduction outside of Egypt.

Facing page: More than 280 species have been sighted at the Stillwater National Wildlife Refuge, 60 miles east of Reno. These wetlands attract more than a quarter million waterfowl, as well as over 20,000 other water birds, annually.

Above: Wild burros on the California/Nevada state line near Death Valley.

Facing page: Cottonwood and wild roses along the Humboldt River.

One can easily imagine being on the moon when viewing
the Volcanic Hills in Fish Lake Valley.

Above: The South Fork canyon of the Owyhee River is 500 to 800 feet deep, narrow, and very meandering.

Facing page: Pyramid Lake exists entirely within the Pyramid Lake Indian Reservation, home to Paiute Indians. PHOTO BY DEON REYNOLDS

Left: Elk are the largest members of the deer family native to Nevada. These cows are in the Schell Creek Range.

Below: Bulrushes and cottonwoods encircle Upper Pahranagut Lake.

Facing page: Sunset on Jeff Davis Peak above Stella Lake at Great Basin National Park.

Cathedral Gorge State Park is located
in a long, narrow valley where erosion has
carved dramatic and unique patterns in
the soft bentonite clay. Trails abound for
exploring the cave-like formations and
cathedral-like spires. Miller Point, a scenic
overlook just north of the park entrance
on U.S. 93, offers excellent views of the
canyon.

Above: The Nevada state capitol building in Carson City was constructed of native sandstone in 1870 at a cost of $100,000. The building combines elements of traditional Corinthian, Ionic, and Doric architecture.

Facing page: Aspen gold in autumn below Wheeler and Jeff Davis peaks at Great Basin National Park.

Above: A backpacker at Valley of Fire traverses cross-bedded Navajo sandstone.

Right: Desert vegetation and stones contrast with the wetlands, pastures, and palm groves at sunrise on a ranch at the head of the Muddy River.

Above: Lupine and mule ears bloom below the aspen in the Jarbidge Wilderness.

Facing page: A moisture-loving plant, this cinquefoil grows along a waterfall above Angel Lake in the East Humboldt Range.

Scott T. Smith is a self-taught photographer whose favorite subject is the natural world. A former research meteorologist, he got his first camera in 1979 and began to take photos on his outdoor adventures—snapshots to share with family and friends. He has been a full-time freelance photographer since 1988, when he quit his "real" job, and he and his wife lived in their truck and the backcountry for a year while making photos.

Scott's images of landscapes, cityscapes, agriculture, natural history, and muscle-powered sports have appeared in text and trade books, calendars, advertising, and magazines, including *Alaska, Audubon, National Parks, Outside,* and *Sierra.* Scott's books include *Nevada: Magnificent Wilderness* and *Along Wyoming's Continental Divide.*

He was selected to participate in "Daybreak 2000," in which 115 photographers worldwide were given 24 hours on January 1, 2000, to capture the first images of the new millennium. In 2003, he shot as a contract pro for "America 24/7," a project which photographers nationwide documented the USA during one week in May.

He and his wife Mary live in Utah's Cache Valley with five pack llamas, a passel of geese, and four spoiled cats.